How to use this workbook

This workbook is to be used together with the book "Master Your Thinking: A Practical Guide to Align Yourself with Reality and Achieve Tangible Results in the Real World"

If you haven't grabbed "Master Your Thinking" yet, you can get it at the URL below:

http://mybook.to/master_thinking

I encourage you to complete all the exercises in this workbook. The more effort you put into it, the better results you'll get.

Let's get started, shall we?

PART I

LETTING GO OF INACCURATE THINKING

Assumption #3:

_____

Write down one limiting assumption you may have adopted from each of the sources below.

Your parents/family:

_____

Your teachers:

_____

Your friends/peers:

_____

The media:

_____

Your experiences:

_____

Your interpretations:

_____

B. Five common biases that distort your thinking

Write down how each bias plays out in your life. Aim to give at least one specific example for each bias below.

One example of self-serving bias:

_____

_____

_____

One example of sunk cost fallacy:

_____

_____

_____

One example of planning fallacy:

One example of survivorship bias:

One example of Dunning-Kruger Effect:

C. How your ego affects your thinking

Write down one specific example for each ego activity below:

One example of living in denial:

_____

_____

_____

What I could do about it:

_____

_____

_____

One example of refusing to ask for help:

_____

_____

_____

What I could do about it:

One example of avoiding failures:

What I could do about it:

One example of blaming other people or external circumstances:

_____

_____

_____

What I could do about it:

_____

_____

_____

D. How your emotions distort your thinking

Complete the exercise below:

- Remember a time when everything felt hopeless or gloomy and you didn't believe you could be happy again. Then realize your negative emotions eventually faded away.
- Think of three current challenges in your life one after the other. How does each one make you feel? Now visualize three things you're grateful for or excited about. Feel better?
- Think of one poor decision you made as a result of negative emotions (anger, hopelessness, frustration etc.) or positive emotions (euphoria).

- For one full minute give yourself some words of encouragement. Remind yourself that you're doing okay, that you have good intentions and that you're proud of all the things you've accomplished. How does it make you feel?

Three common negative thought patterns to avoid

Thought pattern #1—Generalization

Whenever you find yourself generalizing, reframe the sentence to reflect reality more accurately. See examples below:

I'm always late —> I may be late more often than I'd like to be, but I'm also on time on many occasions.

I'm always the one people make fun of —> People might make fun of me occasionally, but I'm certainly not the only one. And it doesn't happen all the time.

I never get things right —> I get things wrong on some occasions, but I get things right many times, too.

Thought pattern #2—All or nothing thinking

Look at each area of your life and see how you may be falling for the all or nothing thinking. Try to come up with specific examples.

Career:

_____

_____

_____

Finance:

Health:

Personal growth:

Relationships:

_____

_____

_____

Spirituality:

_____

_____

_____

Thought pattern #3—Dramatization

Remember one time you worried about something that never happened. Write it down below.

One thing I worried about, but that never happened:

_____

_____

_____

PART II

ALIGNING YOURSELF WITH REALITY

1. Accepting reality as it is

Should vs. could

Write down at least three "should" statements you often use.

Should statement #1:

_____

Should statement #2:

_____

Should statement #3:

_____

Now, replace "should" by "could" for each statement.

Could statement #1:

_____

Could statement #2:

_____

Could statement #3:

_____

See how it makes you feel and how it changes your thought process.

2. Uncovering your assumptions

A. Identifying your assumptions

Select one important goal and make a list of all the assumptions you may be making about it. We'll keep using this goal for future exercises.

Your goal:

_____

Your assumptions:

-

-

-

-

-

-

-

-

-

-

-

-

-

To help you identify your assumptions, please refer to the questions below:

- What are your assumptions regarding the best ways to achieve this goal? What strategies do you assume will work and why?
- Do you think it will be easy or hard and why?
- How long do you think it will take you to reach this goal and why?

B. Testing your assumptions

- Look at the list of assumptions you just wrote down.
- Next to each assumption, write down the accuracy score you would give it on a scale from 1 to 10 (one being completely inaccurate and 10 being one hundred percent accurate).

3. Refining your model of reality

A. Revising your assumptions

What do you know for sure regarding your goal? Write down the assumptions you believe to be correct regarding your goal.

_____

_____

_____

_____

How can you be so certain? Write down the reasons you think you're right.

_____

_____

_____

_____

B. Sharpening your thinking by asking yourself questions

Spend some time answering the questions below to sharpen your thinking.

1) Do I believe I will achieve my goal?

_____

2) Do I have a track record of achieving similar goals?

_____

_____

_____

3) What makes me think I will achieve this goal? What concrete evidence or tangible results are there to support this claim?

———————————————————————————

———————————————————————————

———————————————————————————

4) Do the people around me believe I will achieve my goal?

———————————————————————————

———————————————————————————

———————————————————————————

5) Do I have the energy and/or time required to achieve this goal within the set timeframe?

———————————————————————————

———————————————————————————

———————————————————————————

6) How many people have achieved this goal before? How many people try to achieve it now?

7) Who has achieved that goal before?

8) Why is this goal important to me?

9) If I keep doing what I'm doing every day, will I achieve my goals? If not, what exactly needs to change?

---

10) What are the best approaches/strategies I can follow?

---

11) What does my intuition tell me to do?

C. Interviewing experienced people

Complete at least one of the exercises below (and preferably both).

- Ask each question to the relevant person/people
- Watch interviews/read biographies and try answering the question below based on the information you gathered.

1) How does this work?

_____

_____

_____

2) What are the biggest assumptions you make? And how do you know these are accurate or effective?

_____

_____

_____

3) What do I need to understand that I may not understand yet?

_____

_____

_____

4) If you were in my shoes, what would you do?

_____

_____

_____

5) If you were to start all over again, what would you do to get results faster?

_____

_____

_____

6) If you had to choose only one activity to focus on, which one would give you the best results?

_____

_____

_____

D. Doing your own research

1) How to find high-quality information

What is the highest quality of information out there and where can you find it? Write down your answer below:

_____

_____

_____

2) How to find the right information for *you*

_____

_____

_____

a. Making sure you have a clearly defined goal

Answer the questions below:

What exactly is my goal? What do I hope to create by using this information?

_____

_____

_____

_____

_____

_____

If I could obtain the perfect information that would guarantee I achieve my goal, what would it look like? How would it be structured?

_____

_____

_____

_____

_____

_____

b. Understanding how the information applies to *you*

Does the recommended blueprint, program or advice apply in my specific case?

_____

_____

_____

Do I have the desire to take action on that information? If not, why not? What changes do I need to make?

_____

_____

_____

_____

c. Ensuring the information is up to date

To ensure the information is up to date, you can ask yourself some of the questions below:

Is this information still relevant today?

_____

How can I make sure it actually is?

_____

_____

_____

_____

_____

_____

If I'm unable to answer the two questions above, do I know someone who does have the answer?

E. Being curious

Remain curious by engaging in the following activities:

- Stay up to date by checking out new publications on a regular basis.
- Identify the experts in your industry and follow them.
- Challenge your assumptions regularly and revise your strategy as necessary.
- See how you can apply ideas or strategies in areas that are unrelated to your goal.
- Look for trends and practice predicting what could happen in the coming years.

F. Listening to your emotions

How motivated do you feel about your goal?

What could you do to boost your motivation? Could you reframe your goal, find other reasons to incentivize yourself, or change it?

4. Avoiding common misconceptions and delusional thinking

On a scale from 1 to 10, (1 being irrelevant and 10 being spot on), rate how each of these four misconceptions applies to your specific situation.

Misconception #1—I deserve to be successful

0 _____ 10

Misconception #2—I do great work, therefore, I should be successful

0 _____ 10

Misconception #3—I'm just one breakthrough away

0 _____ 10

Misconception #4—I'm already good enough and don't need to improve

0 _____ 10

5. How to create an effective process

Write down all the things you could do to achieve your goal. Don't censure or limit yourself. Just write everything that comes to mind. Try to produce at least ten to twenty actions.

Things you could do to achieve your goal:

-

-

-

-

-

-

-

-

-

-

-

-

-

-

-

-

-

-

A. Narrowing your options

Complete the following exercises:

- Review the ideas you came up with in the previous exercise.
- Come up with at least three possible strategies by combining some of your ideas.
- For each strategy, take a moment to think of all the things this strategy suggests you should *not* be doing.

Strategy #1:

_____

_____

_____

Things it entails you should *not* be doing:

_____

_____

_____

_____

Strategy #2:

_____

_____

_____

Things it entails you should *not* be doing:

_____

_____

_____

Strategy #3:

_____

_____

_____

Things it entails you should *not* be doing:

_____

_____

_____

_____

B. Putting in place an effective process

Review the strategies you've already identified and select the one you believe to be the best.

Write down the process you think you need to implement to make that strategy work (e.g. what you need to do every day/regularly to maximize your chances for success).

_____

_____

_____

_____

_____

_____

_____

_____

_____

_____

_____

C. Cultivating long-term thinking

Complete the sentence below with as many answers as you can think of:

If I was better at thinking long term I would:

-

-

-

-

-

-

-

How to transition from short-term to long-term thinking

a. Creating a long-term vision

Think of a major goal. Then answer the following questions:

What's the ultimate vision behind your goal?

_____

_____

_____

How can you make that goal even more specific?

_____

_____

_____

Why is that goal so important to you?

_____

_____

_____

What financial, physical, mental and/or emotional benefits will you gain from reaching it?

_____

_____

_____

b. Thinking of your long-term goals often

- create a vision board and put it somewhere you'll see it often
- write down your long-term goal on a piece of paper and put it on your desk or somewhere you'll be able to see it daily, and/or
- read your long-term goal every day/week

c. Dedicating time to focus on the big picture

Carve out time every week to focus on the big picture. To help you do so, go through the list of questions below:

- What am I satisfied with?
- What do I want or need to improve?
- What can I do differently to speed up my progress?
- If I were to start the week all over again, what could I do differently?
- If I keep doing what I've done this week, will I achieve my long-term goal? If not, what changes do I need to make?
- Is my current strategy the best one possible? If not, how can I refine it to make it even better?

- What are the very few things that generate most of my results? Can I focus more on these things?
- What are all the things that haven't proven to be effective so far? Can I get rid of some of them?
- If I only work on one thing next week, month, or this year, what would be best in terms of overall progress?

d. Learning to love the process

Complete the sentence below.

For me, focusing more on the process would mean:

_____

_____

_____

e. Letting go of the fear of missing out

Complete the exercises below:

Write down the area(s) of your life in which you experience fear of missing out.

_____

_____

_____

Select one specific area or goal and write down all the opportunities that actually exist out there. What are all your options? What are all the things you could do?

Your area/goal:

All the options out there/things you could do:

Take a moment to appreciate all the opportunities available to you.

f. Reminding yourself to be patient

Regularly remind yourself that you have time. To do this, you can:

Create your own mantras such as "life is a marathon, not a sprint" or simply "I have time" or "be patient". Then, think of them often, write them down and/or display them on your desk or on your wall.

Watch some of Gary Vaynerchuk's videos on the importance of being patient. Search the following on Youtube

- Gary Vee People Have Forgotten the Art of Patience
- Gary Vee Overnight Success

Visualize everything you've already done in the past few months/years and remind yourself of how much more time you have available.

7-step method to approach any new task

Step 1. Prioritizing your task

Before you start working on a task, ask yourself:

- If I could do only one thing today, which task would have the most impact?
- Is this task moving me closer to my main goal?
- Do I really need to do it right now, or can I do it later?

Step 2. Assessing the validity of your task

To ensure the task is something you actually need to do, ask yourself the following questions:

- Do I really need to do this task?
- Is right now the best time? What would happen if I delay it for a week? A month? Forever?
- Do I need to do this task, or am I doing it because it makes me feel good? In short, am I working on this task to escape from what I really should be doing?

Step 3. Clarifying what needs to be done

Before working on a task, be certain you know exactly what is required. Therefore before starting any task ask yourself:

- What exactly do I need to do here?
- What am I trying to accomplish?
- What does the finished product look like?

Step 4. Determining whether you should be the person doing it

You have strengths, but you also have weaknesses. Whenever possible, try to delegate any task someone else can do better, faster or more cheaply than you. Ask yourself the following questions:

- Is this task really worth my time?
- Can someone else do it better than me? If so, can I ask for help?
- What would happen if I simply remove/postpone this task?
- Do I enjoy working on this task? Does it motivate me?

Step 5. Finding out the most effective way to tackle a task

Just taking a few minutes to work out the best way to approach a task can save you so much time. Ask yourself the following questions:

- What tool(s) can I use, people can I ask, or method can I rely on to complete this task as efficiently and effectively as possible?
- What skill(s) could I learn or improve to help me complete this task faster in the future?

Step 6. Batching the task with other similar tasks

- Can I batch this task with other similar tasks to boost my productivity?

Step 7. Automating/systemizing your task

- Can I create templates to reuse every time I work on this or on similar tasks?
- Can I create a checklist?

PART III

EMPOWERING YOUR MODEL OF REALITY

I. Design an empowering environment

A. Changing your peer group

Answer the following questions:

Who do I want to spend more time with?

_____

_____

_____

Who do I want to spend less time with?

_____

_____

_____

Who are the people who have already achieved the goals I seek to achieve?

_____

_____

_____

Where can I find these positive and supportive people?

_____

_____

_____

1) How to protect yourself from negative people

Make a list of all the people who are having a negative impact on your life:

-

-

-

-

-

-

Answer the following question: How likely am I to achieve my goal if I hang out with the same people?

_____

_____

_____

2) Surround yourself with people who will support you

a. Join groups of like-minded people

What group or groups could you join? Who could you contact?

_____

_____

_____

b. Create your own event

Who do you want to attract into your life and what kind of event could you organize that would appeal to them?

_____

_____

_____

c. Look for a mentor/d. Hire a coach

If necessary, start looking for a mentor or a coach.

B. Change your physical environment

What one thing could you do to spend more time with people who will support your goal?

_____

_____

_____

What one thing could you do to create a more positive environment to motivate you to work on your goal?

_____

_____

_____

What one thing could you do to optimize your current environment and make it easier to work on your goal?

_____

_____

_____

C. Optimizing your digital environment

Optimize your digital environment by:

- Turning off phone notifications
- Checking your emails as few times as possible (if possible, limit your email access to once or twice per day)
- Turning off WIFI or staying away from social media or any other sources of online distraction (e.g. install software to remove distractions as and when necessary)
- Unsubscribing from newsletters

2. Developing unshakeable confidence

A. Understanding belief

Remember the following when it comes to cultivating belief:

1. Not possible —> 2. possible —> 3. probable —> 4. inevitable

B. Adopting key empowering beliefs

Print out the page with the five beliefs at the end of this action guide and read them on a regular basis. Think of them often. If you identify other great beliefs you want to adopt, add them to your repertoire. As a reminder, the five beliefs are:

1. I can always improve over the long term
2. If someone else can, I can
3. If I can do it once, I can do it again
4. Others will give up, therefore, I will succeed
5. Success is inevitable

C. Achieving goals consistently

Complete the exercises below:

- Re-using the goal you've been working with, break it down into yearly, monthly, weekly and daily goals.
- For the next thirty days, set three simple daily tasks and make sure you complete them.

Your goal:

_____

Now break it down as below

Yearly goals:

-

-

-

Monthly goals:

-

-

-

Weekly goals:

-

-

-

Daily goals:

-

-

-

D. Conditioning your mind

1) Using affirmations

Create your own affirmations using these tips:

- **State your affirmation in the present tense.**
- **Avoid using negatives** and say your affirmation in the positive form. For instance, say "I'm courageous" rather than "I'm no longer afraid."
- **Aim to change your physiological state.** Engage your body and experiment with different vocal tones. This will add power to your affirmation.
- **Use the power of visualization.** See yourself in specific situations that relate to your affirmation, then try to feel as though you already have what you want. Engaging your emotions this way will make your affirmation significantly more powerful.

Write down your own affirmations below:

-

-

-

-

2) Changing your self-talk

Write down a few sentences you can use as positive self-talk to overcome some of the limiting beliefs you hold relating to your goal.

Your limiting belief #1:

_____

Your positive self-talk:

_____

_____

_____

Your limiting belief #2:

_____

Your positive self-talk:

_____

_____

_____

Your limiting belief #3:

_____

Your positive self-talk:

_____

_____

_____

3) Practicing visualization

Spend a few minutes every morning visualizing yourself moving toward your goal and accomplishing it. Additionally, think about your goals throughout your day.

E. Cultivating self-compassion

Complete the exercises below:

- Undertake a seven-day self-compassion challenge.
- Whenever you notice you start beating yourself up, change your self-talk. Tell yourself you're doing okay. Encourage yourself. Be kind to yourself.

3. Expand your field of possibilities

A. Generating luck

1) Refusing to believe in luck

Answer the following question:

If there wasn't such a thing as luck, what would you do differently to improve the chances you achieve your goal? Write down everything that comes to mind:

_____

_____

_____

_____

2) Repeatedly thinking about what you want

Spend a few minutes focusing on what you want every day. I recommend you focus on your goal twice (first thing when you wake and before going to bed).

3) Broadcasting your desires to the world

What is one specific thing you could do to broadcast your goal to people who could potentially help you achieve it?

_____

_____

_____

4) Taking consistent action in line with a clearly defined strategy

Make sure you take consistent action toward your goal. These actions should be the ones you identified in 5. *How to create an effective process, B. Putting in place an effective process.*

5) Learning as much as you can from the feedback you receive from reality

Make sure you learn from every setback you face. Ask yourself, what's great about it? What can I learn from that situation?

B. Asking yourself empowering questions

Answer the questions below:

How can I achieve my goal? What can I do to help myself reach it?

What if I could achieve my goal? What if it was possible?

C. Taking consistent action

1) The benefits of taking action

Answer the following questions:

How well is my current approach working for me?

Am I really taking enough action to reach my goal?

_____

_____

_____

What would taking massive action mean to me?

_____

_____

_____

2) Doubling down on what works

Answer the following questions:

What if anything is bringing me the best results?

_____

_____

_____

What could I do to double down on that success?

_____

_____

_____

_____

D. Leveraging the power of gratitude

Practice one of the exercises below for at least fourteen days:

- Write down things you're grateful for.
- Thank people who crossed your life.
- Focus on one object and appreciate its existence.
- Listen to gratitude songs/guided meditation.

5 Key Empowering Beliefs

Look at the following empowering beliefs as often as possible. Read them. Say them out loud. Think about them and what they mean exactly to you.

1. I can always improve over the long term
2. If someone else can, I can
3. If I can do it once, I can do it again
4. Others will give up, therefore, I will succeed
5. Success is inevitable

Conclusion

I hope you benefited from this workbook and will achieve most or all your goals and dreams in the coming years.

Let me wish you all the best with your new endeavors. I'm very much looking forward to hearing from you.

If you have any questions send me an email at:

thibaut.meurisse@gmail.com

NOTE:

67

Master Your Life With The Mastery Series

If you haven't yet, you can check the other books in the **Mastery Series**. At the following URL:

mybook.to/Master_Emotions

To read a preview of *Master Your Emotions,* turn the page.

MASTER YOUR EMOTIONS (PREVIEW)

The mind in its own place, and in itself can make a heaven of Hell, a hell of Heaven.

— JOHN MILTON, POET.

We all experience a wild range of emotions throughout our lives. I had to admit, while writing this book, I experienced highs and lows myself. At first, I was filled with excitement and thrilled at the idea of providing people with a guide to help them understand their emotions. I imagined how readers' lives would improve as they learned to control their emotions. My motivation was high and I couldn't help but imagine how great the book would be.

Or so I thought.

After the initial excitement, the time came to sit down to write the actual book, and that's when the excitement wore off pretty quickly. Ideas that looked great in my mind suddenly felt dull. My writing seemed boring, and I felt as though I had nothing substantive or valuable to contribute.

Sitting at my desk and writing became more challenging each day. I started losing confidence. Who was I to write a book about emotions if I couldn't even master my own emotions? How ironic! I considered giving up. There are already plenty of books on the topic, so why add one more?

At the same time, I realized this book was a perfect opportunity to work on my own emotional issues. And who doesn't suffer from negative emotions from time to time? We all have highs and lows, don't we? The key is what we *do* with our lows. Are we using our emotions to grow? Are we learning something from them? Or are we beating ourselves up over them?

So, let's talk about *your* emotions now. Let me start by asking you this:

How do you feel right now?

Knowing how you feel is the first step toward taking control of your emotions. You may have spent so much time internalizing you've lost touch with your emotions. Perhaps you answered as follows: "I feel this book could be useful," or "I really feel I could learn something from this book."

However, none of these answers reflect how you feel. You don't 'feel like this,' or 'feel like that,' you simply 'feel.' You don't 'feel like' this book could be useful, you 'think' this book could be useful, and that generates an emotion which makes you 'feel' excited about reading it. Feelings manifest as physical sensations in your body, not as an idea in your mind. Perhaps, the reason the word 'feel' is so often overused or misused is because we don't want to talk about our emotions.

So, how do you feel now?

Why is it important to talk about emotions?

How you feel determines the quality of your life. Your emotions can make your life miserable or truly magical. That's why they are among the most important things to focus on. Your emotions color all your experiences. When you feel good, everything seems, feels, or tastes better. You also think better thoughts. Your energy levels are higher and possibilities seem limitless. Conversely, when you feel depressed, everything seems dull. You have little energy and you become unmotivated. You feel stuck in a place (mentally and physically) you don't want to be, and the future looks gloomy.

Your emotions can also act as a powerful guide. They can tell you something is wrong and allow you to make changes in your life. As such, they may be among the most powerful personal growth tools you have.

Sadly, neither your teachers nor your parents taught you how emotions work or how to control them. I find it ironic that just about anything comes with a how-to manual, while your mind doesn't. You've never received an instruction manual to teach you how your mind works and how to use it to better manage your emotions, have you? I haven't. In fact, until now, I doubt one even existed.

What you'll learn in this book

This book is the how-to manual your parents should have given you at birth. It's the instruction manual you should have received at school. In it, I'll share everything you need to know about emotions so you can overcome your fears and limitations and become the type of person you really want to be.

You'll learn what emotions are, how they are formed, and how you can use them for your personal growth. You'll also learn how to deal with negative emotions and condition your mind to create more positive emotions.

It is my sincere hope and expectation that, by the end of this book, you will have a clear understanding of what emotions are and will have all the tools you need to start taking control of them.

More specifically, this book will help you:

- Understand what emotions are and how they impact your life
- Identify negative emotions that control your life and learn to overcome them
- Change your story to take better control over your life and create a more compelling future, and
- Reprogram your mind to experience more positive emotions.

Here is a more detailed summary of what you'll learn in this book:

In **Part I**, we'll discuss what emotions are. You'll learn why you are wired to focus on negativity and what you can do to counter this effect. You'll also discover how your beliefs impinge upon your emotions. Finally, you'll learn how negative emotions work and why they are so tricky.

In **Part II**, we'll go over the things that directly impact your emotions. You'll understand the roles your body, your thoughts, your words, or your sleep, play in your life and how you can use them to change your emotions.

In **Part III**, you'll learn how emotions are formed. You'll also learn how to condition your mind to experience more positive emotions.

And finally, in **Part IV**, we'll discuss how to use your emotions as a tool for personal growth. You'll learn why you experience emotions such as fear or depression and how they work. You'll then discover how to use them to grow.

I. What emotions are

Have you ever wondered what emotions are and what purpose they serve?

In this section, we'll discuss how your survival mechanism affects your emotions. Then, we'll explain what the 'ego' is and how it impacts your emotions. Finally, we'll discover the mechanism behind emotions and learn why negative emotions can be so hard to deal with.

1. How your survival mechanism affects your emotions

Why people have a bias towards negativity

Your brain is designed for survival, which explains why you're able to read this book at this very moment. When you think about it, the probability of you being born was extremely low. For this miracle to happen, all the generations before you had to survive long enough to procreate. In their quest for survival and procreation, they must have faced death hundreds or perhaps thousands of times.

Fortunately, unlike your ancestors, you're (probably) not facing death every day. In fact, in many parts of the world, life has never been safer. Yet, your survival mechanism hasn't changed much. Your brain still scans your environment looking for potential threats.

In many ways, some parts of your brain have become obsolete. While you may not be seconds away from being eaten by a predator, your brain still gives significantly more weight to negative events than to positive ones.

Fear of rejection is one example of a bias toward negativity. In the past, being rejected from your tribe would reduce your chances of survival significantly. Therefore, you learned to look for any sign of rejection, and this became hardwired in your brain.

Nowadays, being rejected often carries little or no consequence to your long-term survival. You could be hated by the entire world and still have a job, a roof and plenty of food on the table, yet, your brain is still programmed to perceive rejection as a threat to your survival.

This is why rejection can be so painful. While you know most rejections are no big deal, you nevertheless feel the emotional pain. If you listen to your mind, you may even create a whole drama around it. You may believe you aren't worthy of love and dwell on a rejection for days or weeks. Worse still, you may become depressed as a result of this rejection.

In fact, one single criticism can often outweigh hundreds of positive ones. That's why, an author with fifty 5-star reviews, is likely to feel terrible when they receive a single 1-star review. While the author understands the 1-star review isn't a threat to her survival, her authorial brain doesn't. It likely interprets the negative review as a threat to her ego which triggers an emotional reaction.

The fear of rejection can also lead you to over-dramatize events. If your boss criticized you at work, your brain may see the event as a threat and you now think, "What if I'm fired? What if I can't find a job quickly enough and my wife leaves me? What about my kids? What if I can't see them again?"

While you are fortunate to have such an effective survival mechanism, it is also your responsibility to separate real threats from imaginary ones. If you don't, you'll experience unnecessary pain and worry that will negatively impact the quality of your life. To overcome this bias towards negativity, you must reprogram your mind. One of a human being's greatest powers is our ability to use our thoughts to shape our reality and interpret events in a more empowering way. This book will teach you how to do this.

Why your brain's job isn't to make you happy

Your brain's primary job is not to make you happy, but to ensure your survival. Thus, if you want to be happy, you must take control of your emotions rather than hoping you'll be happy because it's your natural state. In the following section, we'll discuss what happiness is and how it works.

How dopamine can mess with your happiness

Dopamine is a neurotransmitter which, among other functions, plays a major role in rewarding certain behaviors. When dopamine is released into specific areas of your brain—the pleasure centers—you get a high. This is what happens during exercise, when you gamble, have sex, or eat great food.

One of the roles of dopamine is to ensure you look for food so you don't die of starvation, and you search for a mate so you can reproduce. Without dopamine, our species would likely be extinct by now. It's a pretty good thing, right?

Well, yes and no. In today's world, this reward system is, in many cases, obsolete. While in the past, dopamine was linked to our survival instinct, The release of dopamine can now be generated artificially. A great example of this effect is social media, which uses psychology to suck as much time as possible out of your life. Have you noticed all these notifications that pop up constantly? They're used to trigger a release of dopamine so you stay connected, and the longer you stay connected, the more money the services make. Watching pornography or gambling also leads to a release of dopamine which can make these activities highly addictive.

Fortunately, we don't need to act each time our brain releases dopamine. For instance, we don't need to constantly check our Facebook newsfeeds just because it gives us a pleasurable shot of dopamine.

Today's society is selling a version of happiness that can make us *un*happy. We've become addicted to dopamine largely because of marketers who have found effective ways to exploit our brains. We receive multiple shots of dopamine throughout the day and we love it. But is that the same thing as happiness?

Worse than that, dopamine can create real addictions with severe consequences on our health. Research conducted at Tulane University showed that, when given permission to self-stimulate their pleasure center, participants did it an average of forty times per minute. They chose the stimulation of their pleasure center over food, even refusing to eat when hungry!

Korean, Lee Seung Seop is an extreme case of this syndrome. In 2005, Mr Seop died after playing a video game for fifty-eight hours straight with very little food or water, and no sleep. The subsequent investigation concluded the cause of death was heart failure induced by exhaustion and dehydration. He was only twenty-eight years old.

To take control of your emotions, it is essential you understand the role dopamine plays and how it affects your happiness. Are you addicted to your phone? Are you glued to your TV? Or maybe you spend too much time playing video games. Most of us are addicted to something. For some people it's obvious, but for others, it's more subtle. For instance, you could be addicted to thinking. To better control your emotions, it is important to shed the light on your addictions as they can rob you of your happiness.

The 'one day I will' myth

Do you believe that one day you will achieve your dream and finally be happy? This is unlikely to happen. You may (and I hope you will) achieve your dream, but you won't live 'happily ever after.' This is just another trick your mind plays on you.

Your mind quickly acclimates to new situations, which is probably the result of evolution and our need to adapt continually in order to survive and reproduce. This is also probably why the new car or house you want will only make you happy for a while. Once the initial excitement wears off, you'll move on to crave the next exciting thing. This phenomenon is known as 'hedonic adaptation.'

How hedonic adaptation works

Let me share an interesting study that will likely change the way you see happiness. This study, which was conducted on lottery winners and paraplegics, was extremely eye-opening for me. Conducted in 1978, the investigation evaluated how winning the lottery or becoming a paraplegic influence happiness:

The study found that one year after the event, both groups were just as happy as they were beforehand. Yes, just as happy (or unhappy). You can find more about it by watching Dan Gilbert's Ted Talk, The Surprising Science of Happiness.

Perhaps you believe that you'll be happy once you've 'made it.' But, as the above study on happiness shows, this is simply not true. No matter what happens to you, you'll revert back to your predetermined level of happiness once you've adapted to the new event. This is how your mind works.

Does that mean you can't be happier than you are right now? No. What it means is that, in the long run, external events have very little impact upon your level of happiness.

In fact, according to Sonja Lyubomirsky, author of *The How of Happiness*, fifty percent of our happiness is determined by genetics, forty percent by internal factors, and only ten percent by external factors. These external factors include such things as whether we're single or married, rich or poor, and similar social influences.

This suggests, only ten percent of your happiness is linked to external factors, which is probably way less than you thought. The bottom line is this: Your attitude towards life influences your happiness, not what happens to you.

By now, you understand how your survival mechanism impacts negatively your emotions and prevent you from experiencing more joy and happiness in your life. In the next segment/section we'll learn about the ego.

To read more visit my author page at:

amazon.com/author/thibautmeurisse

ABOUT THE AUTHOR

Thibaut Meurisse is a author, coach, and founder of whatispersonaldevelopment.org.

He has been featured on major personal development websites such as Lifehack, TinyBuddha, MotivationGrid, PickTheBrain, DumbLittleMan or FinerMinds.

Obsessed with self-improvement and fascinated by the power of the brain, his personal mission is to help people realize their full potential and reach higher levels of fulfillment and consciousness.

You can connect with him on his Facebook page

https://www.facebook.com/whatispersonaldevelopment.org

Learn more about Thibaut at

amazon.com/author/thibautmeurisse

Made in the USA
Monee, IL
19 May 2020